Complete Uses of a

DEAD • CAT

A Hundred and One Uses of a Dead Cat
A Hundred and One More Uses of a Dead Cat
Uses of a Dead Cat in History

SIMON BOND

methuen

3 5 7 9 10 8 6 4 2

Published in 2004 by Methuen Publishing Ltd
215 Vauxhall Bridge Rd, London SW1V 1EJ

A Hundred and One Uses of a Dead Cat first published in 1981 by Eyre Methuen Ltd
A Hundred and One More Uses of a Dead Cat first published in 1982 by Methuen London Ltd
Uses of a Dead Cat in History first published in 1992 by Mandarin Paperbacks

This collection first published in 2001 by Methuen Publishing Limited.
Reissued with a new cover in 2004.

Methuen Publishing Limited Reg. No. 3543167

A CIP catalogue record for this book is available from the British Library

ISBN 0 413 76040 5

Printed and bound in Great Britain by
St Edmundsbury Press Ltd, Bury St Edmunds, Suffolk

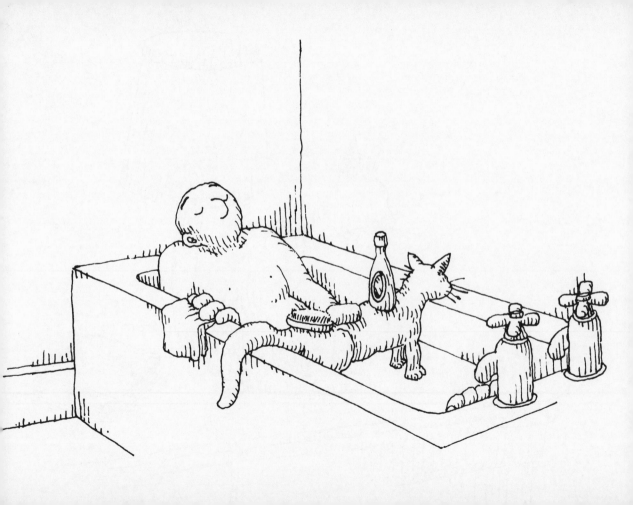

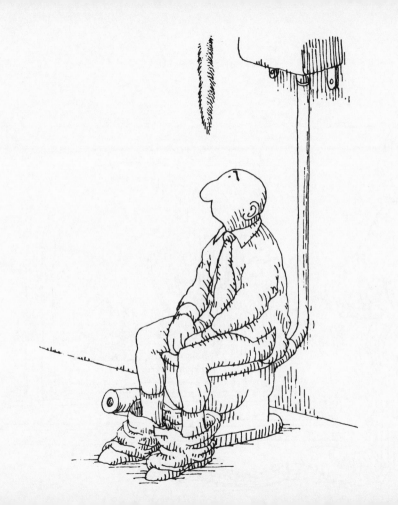

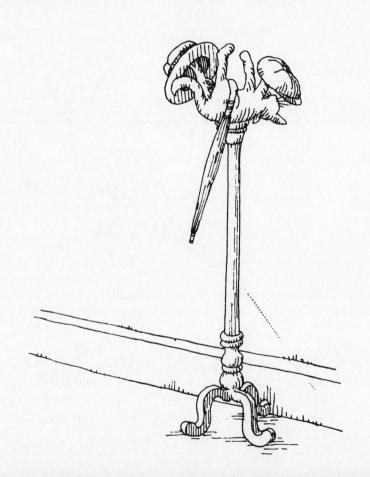

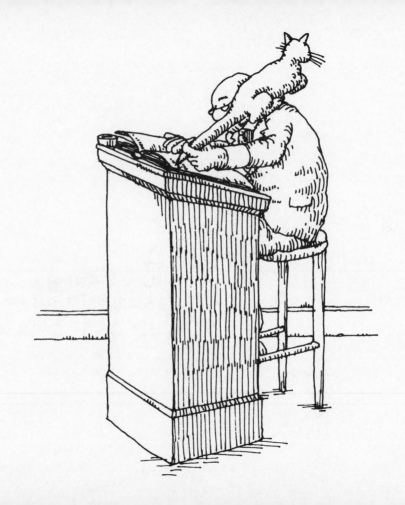

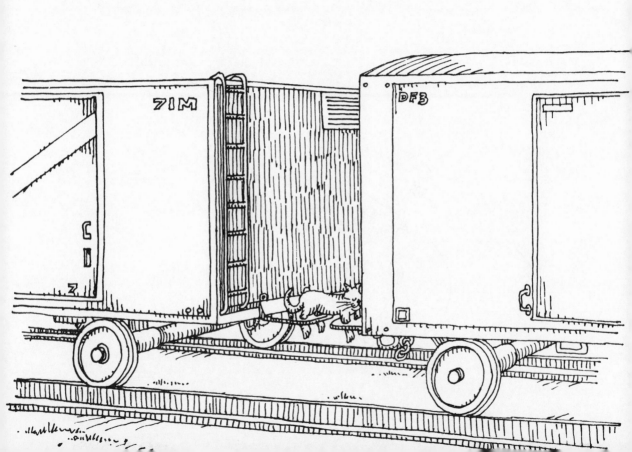

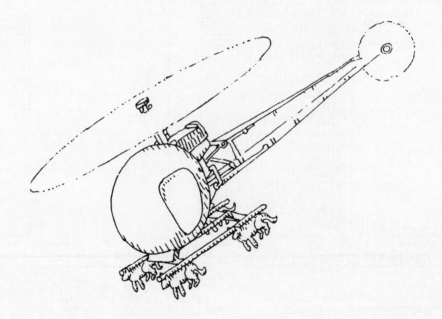

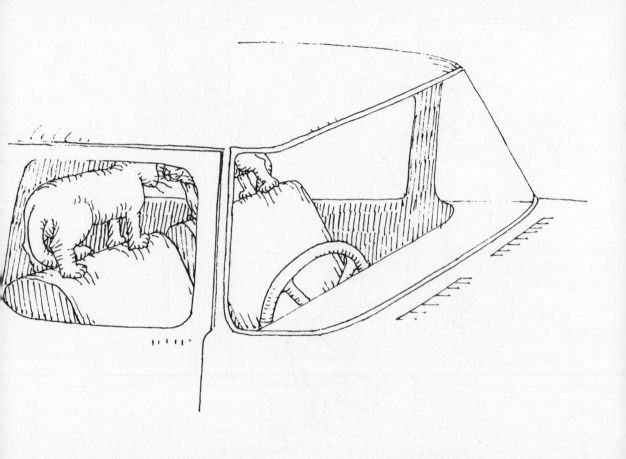

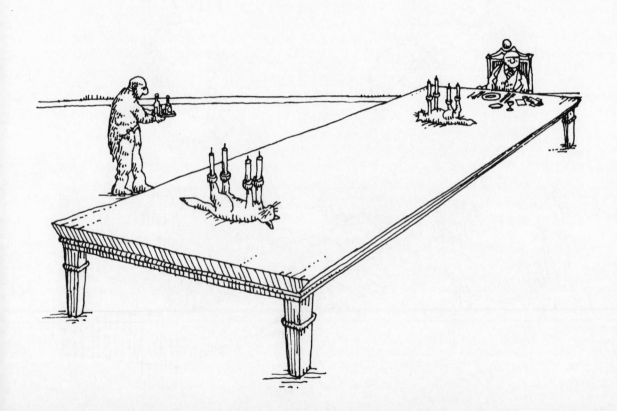

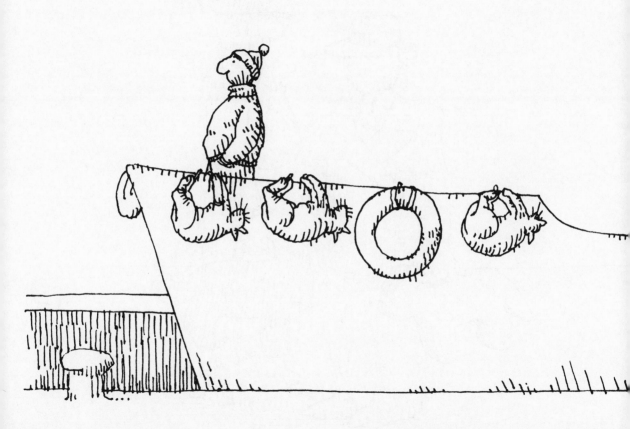

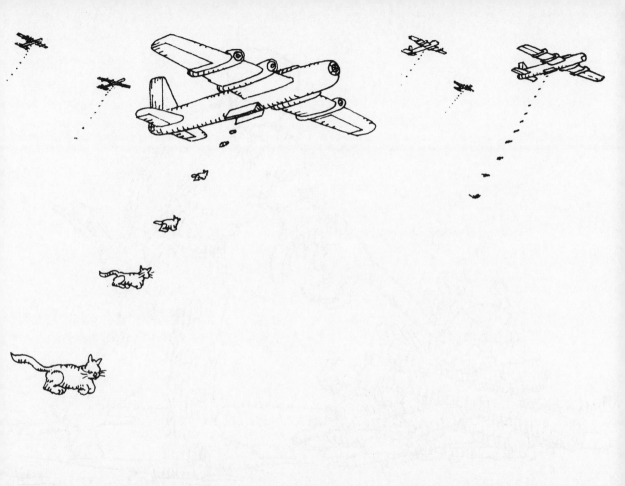

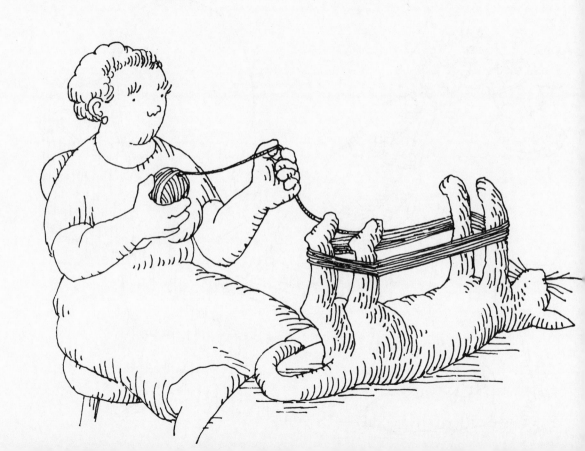

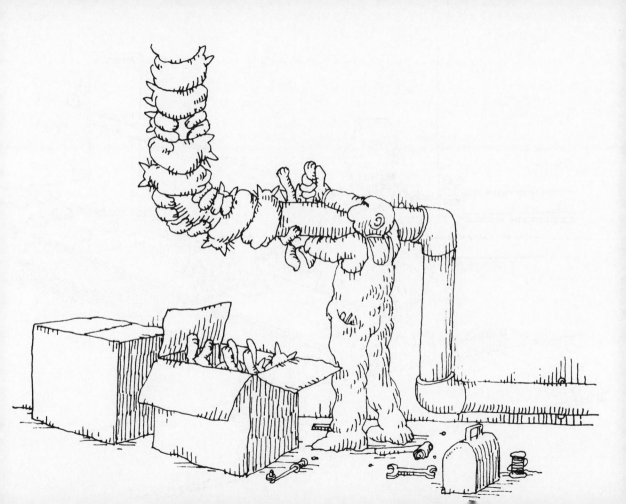

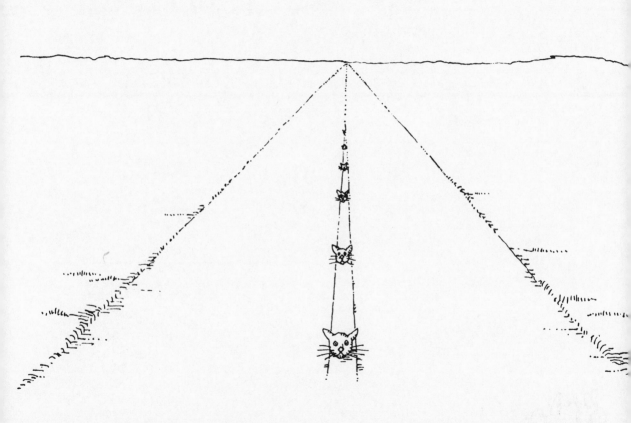

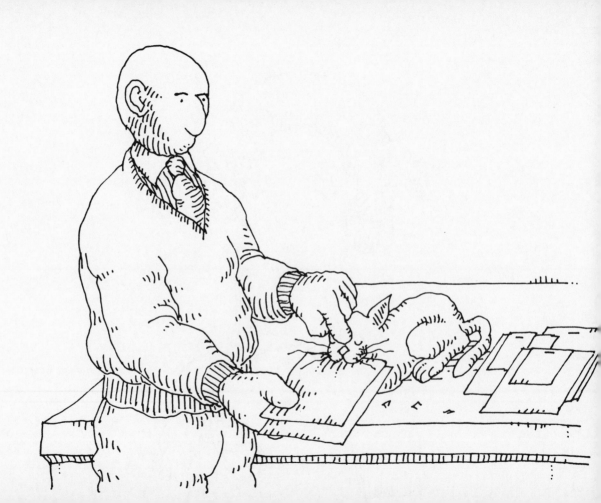

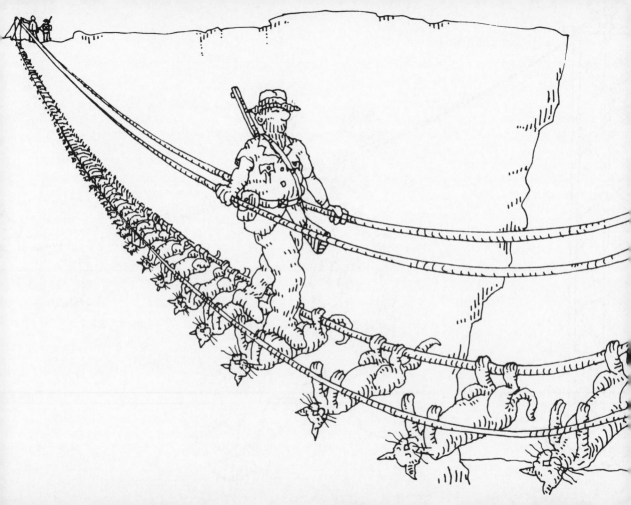

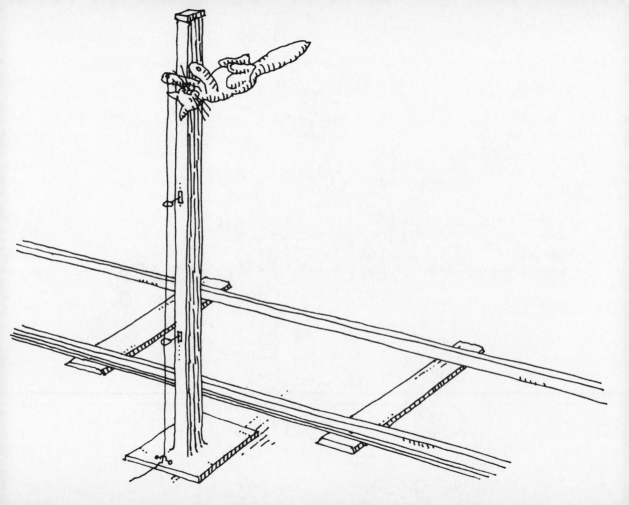

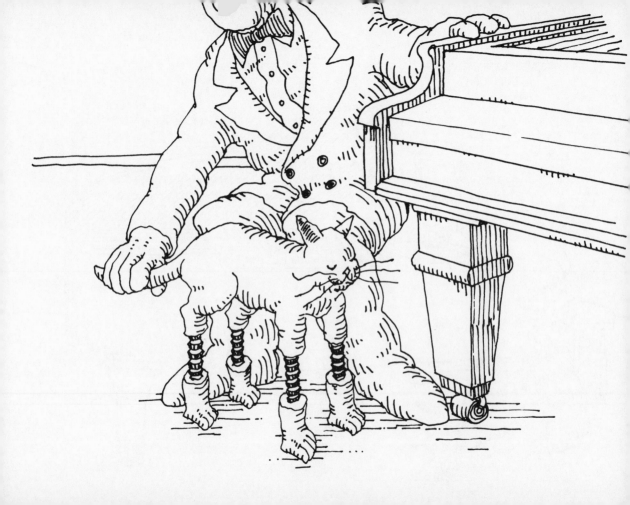

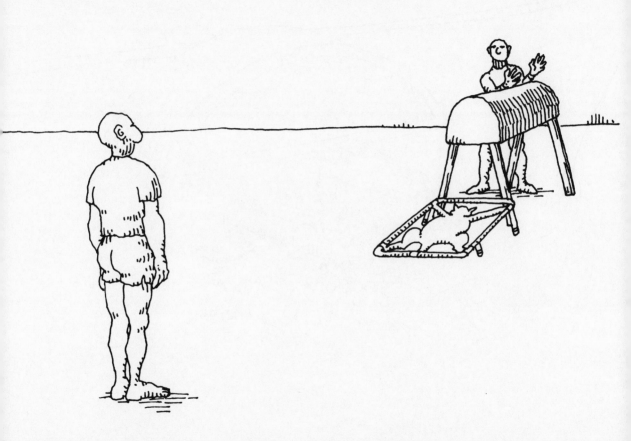

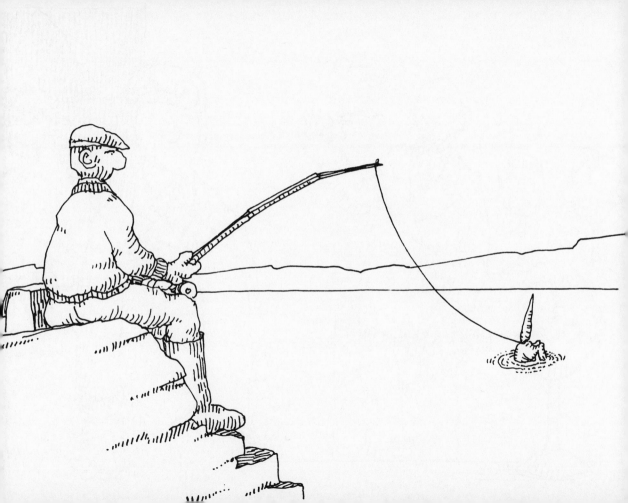

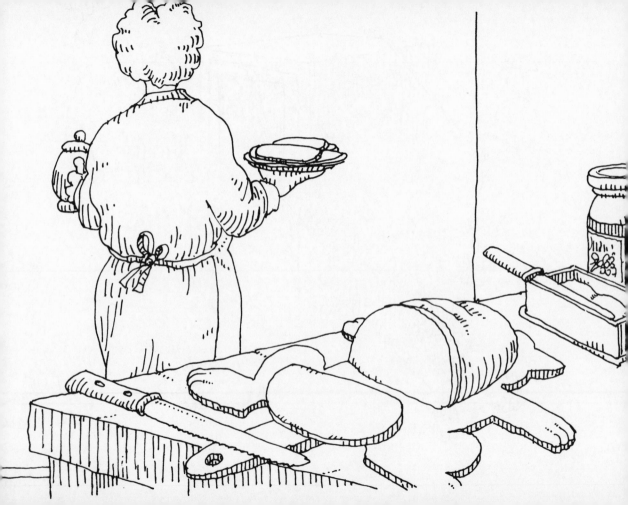

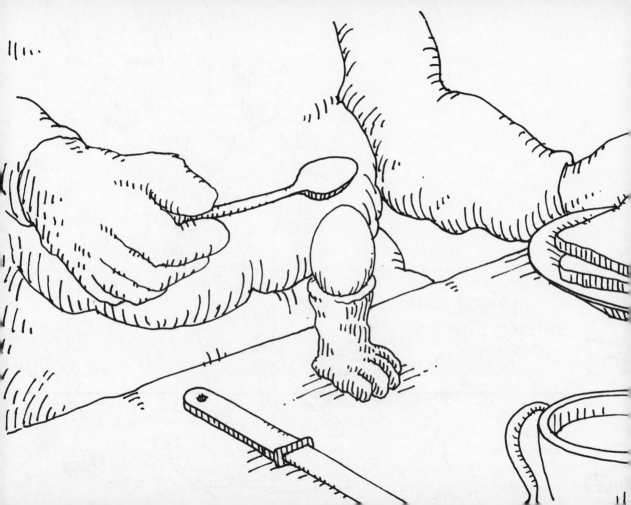

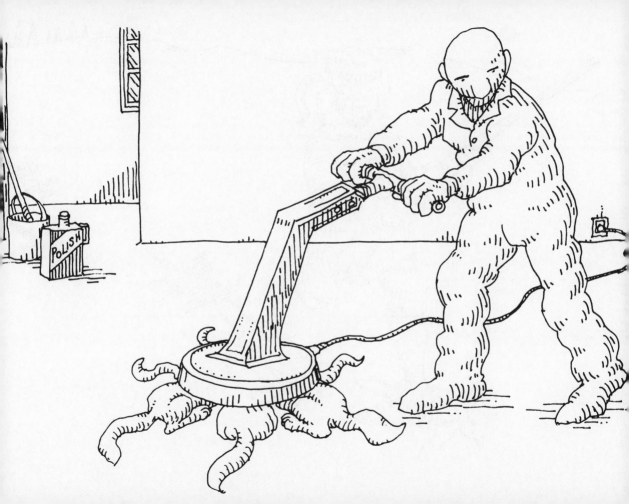

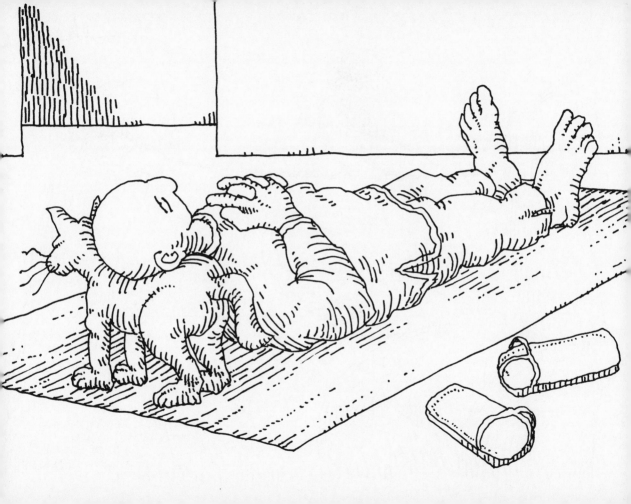

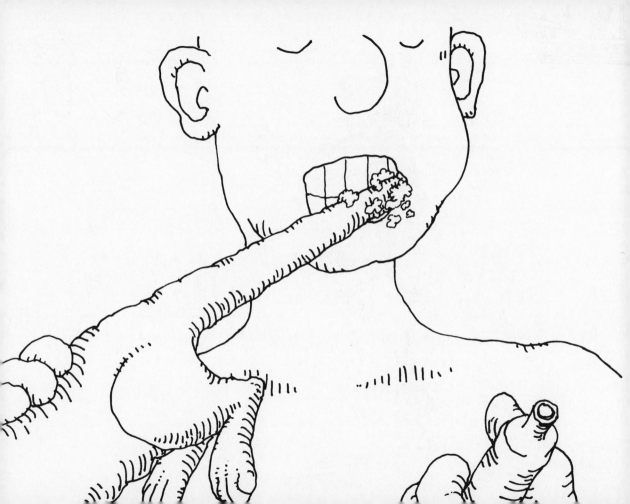

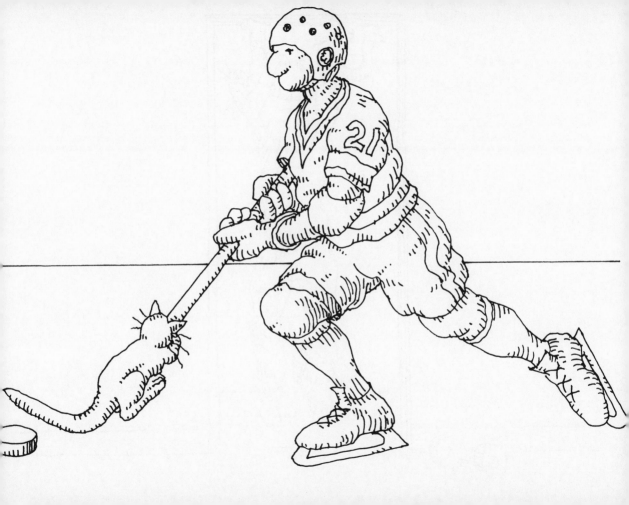

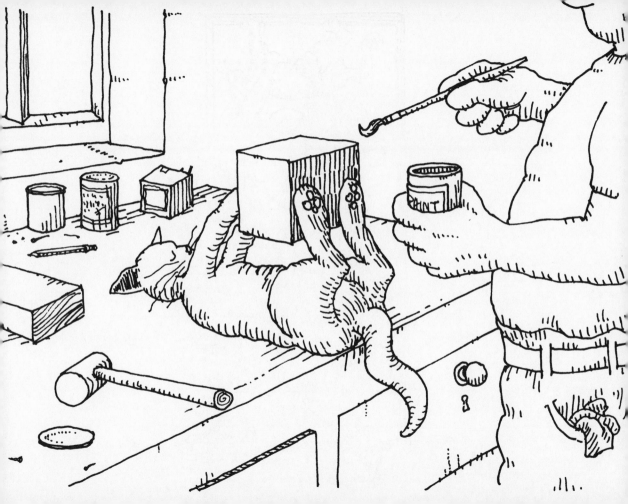

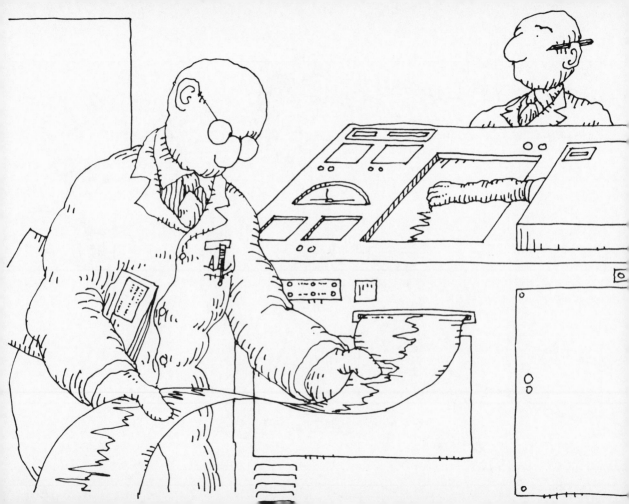

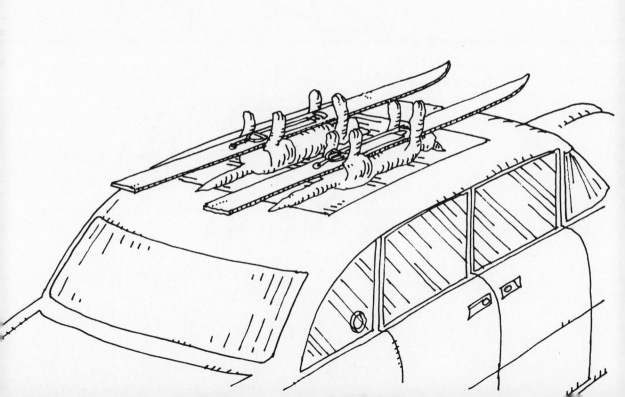

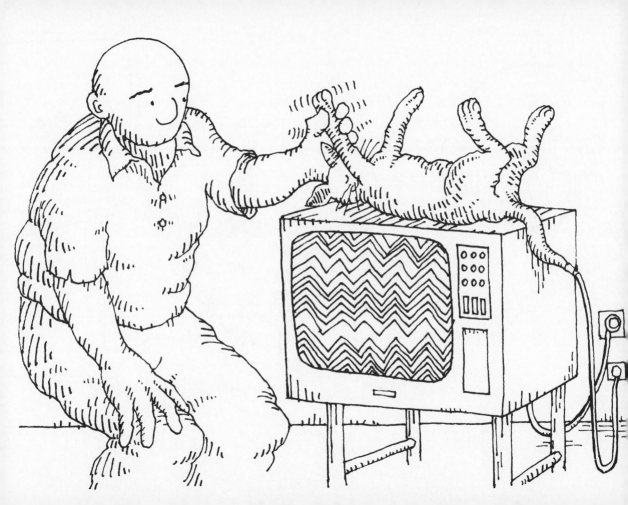

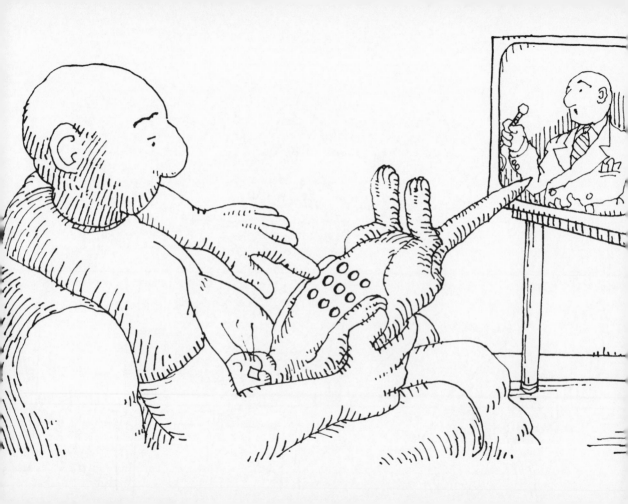

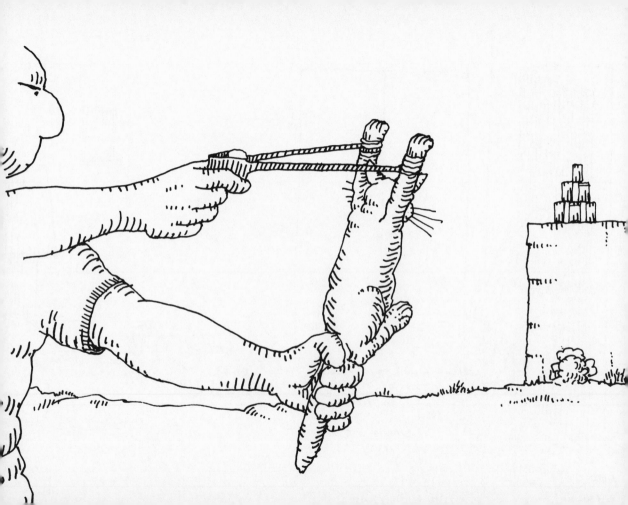

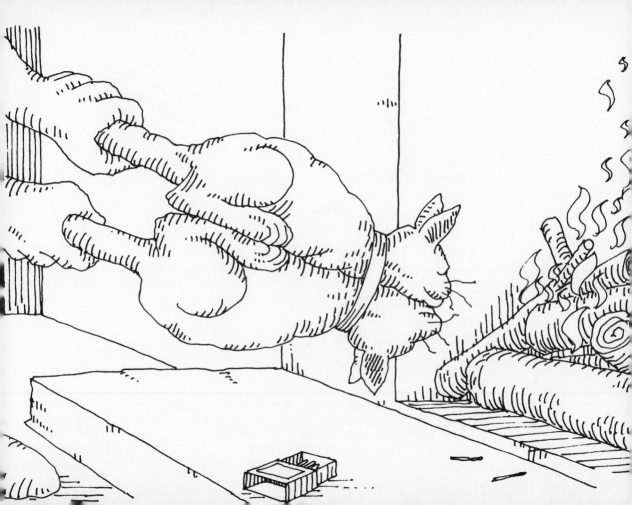

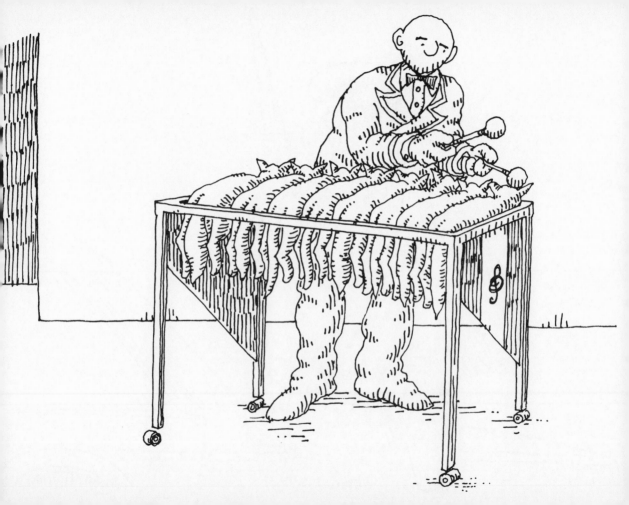

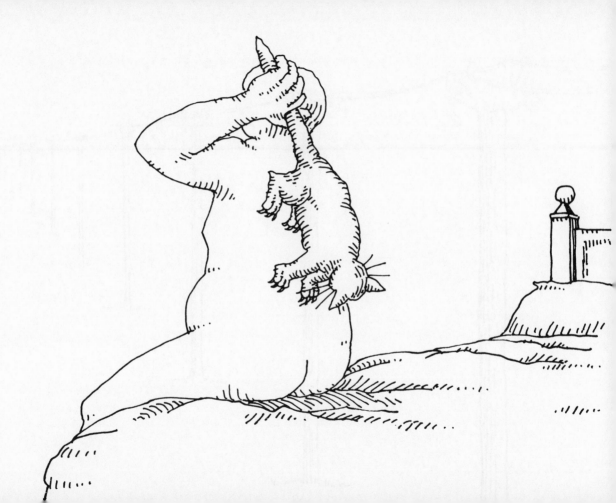

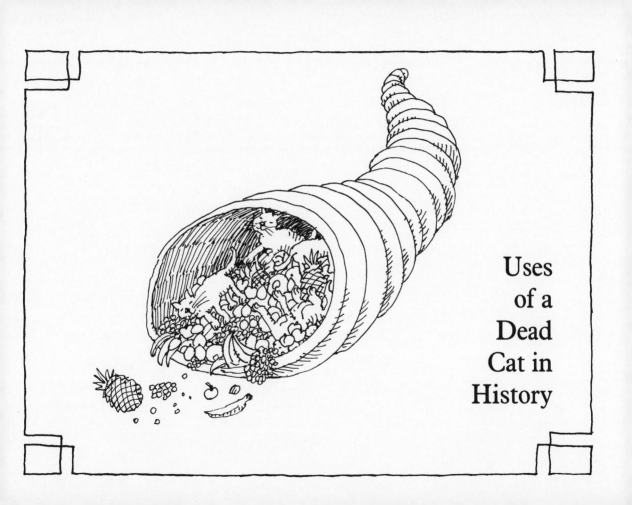

Uses
of a
Dead
Cat in
History

THE ORIGINAL CAST

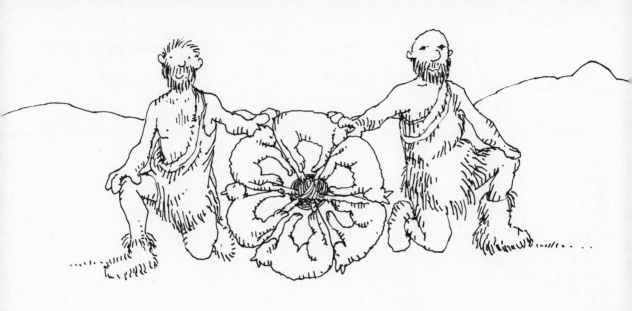

NERG AND OOMA INVENT THE WHEEL

THERE ARE OFTEN INNOCENT VICTIMS.

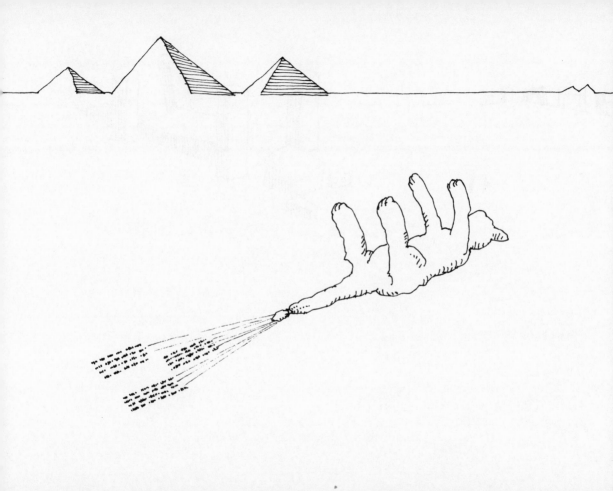

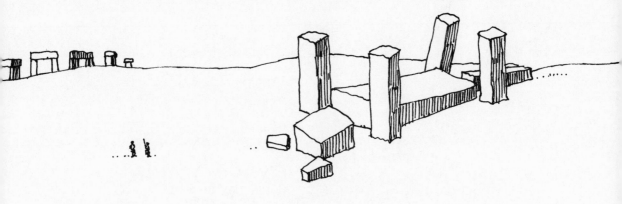

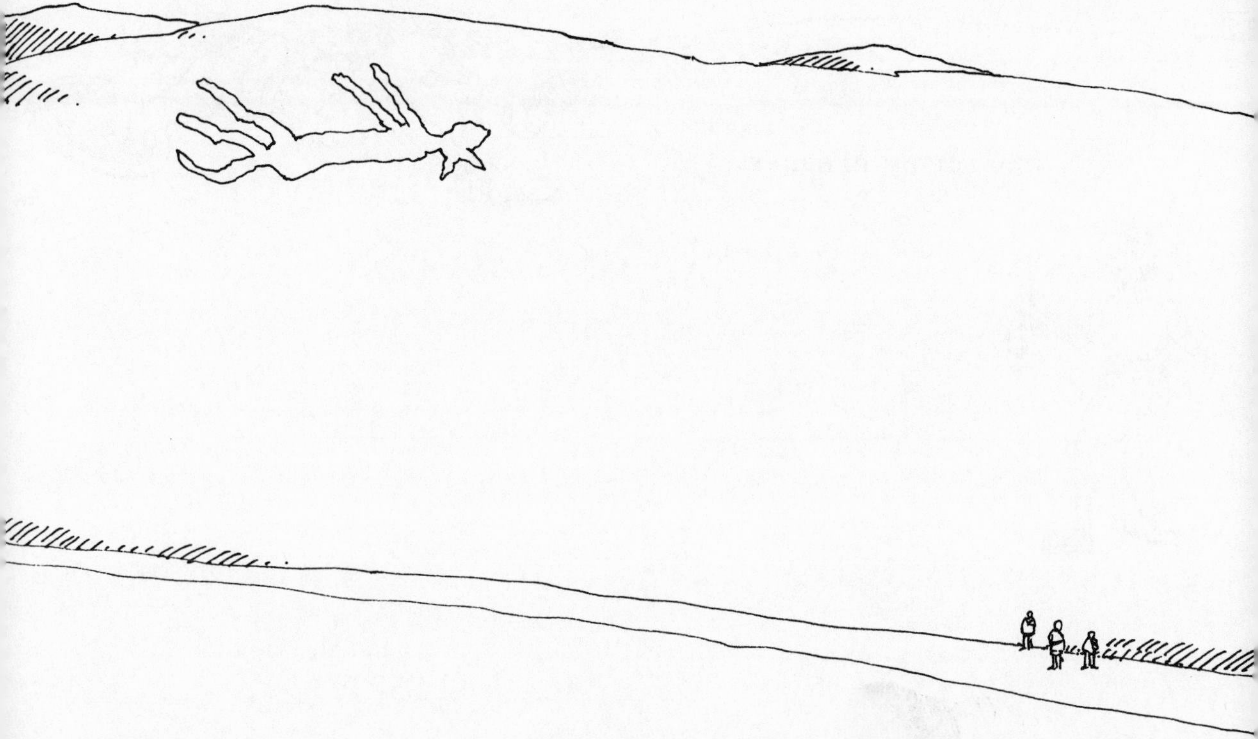

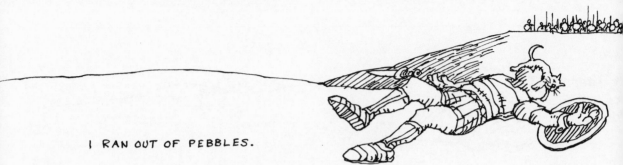

I RAN OUT OF PEBBLES.

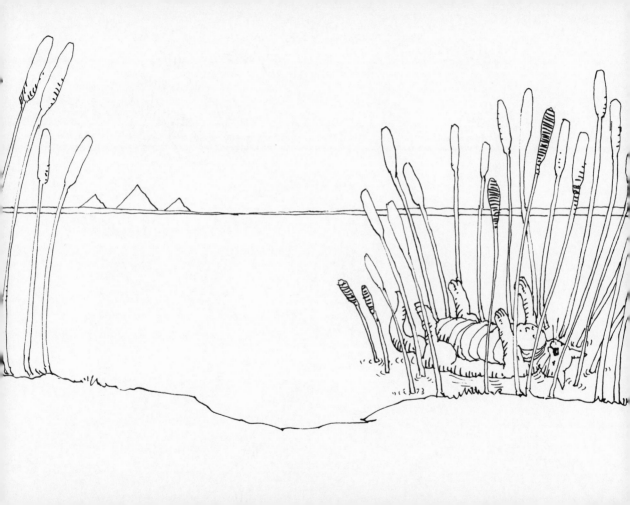

AND AFTER THE PLAGUE OF LOCUSTS...

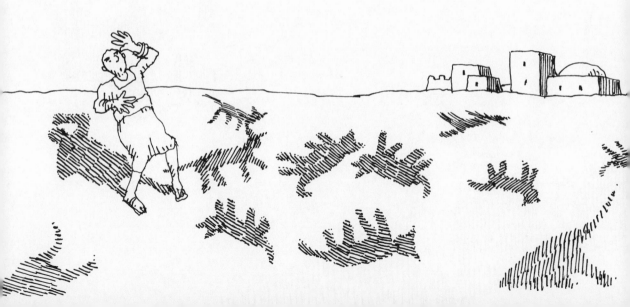

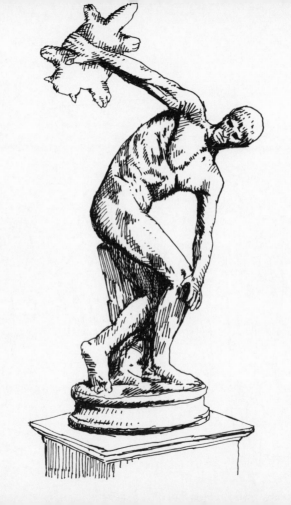

ET TU FLUFFY? 44 BC

JESUS HAS A PRACTICE
BEFORE RAISING LAZARUS

'I think you'd better do the fish again.'

1493

CHRISTOPHER COLUMBUS DISCOVERS
A USE FOR THE POTATO

'They don't roll very well, Sir Francis.'

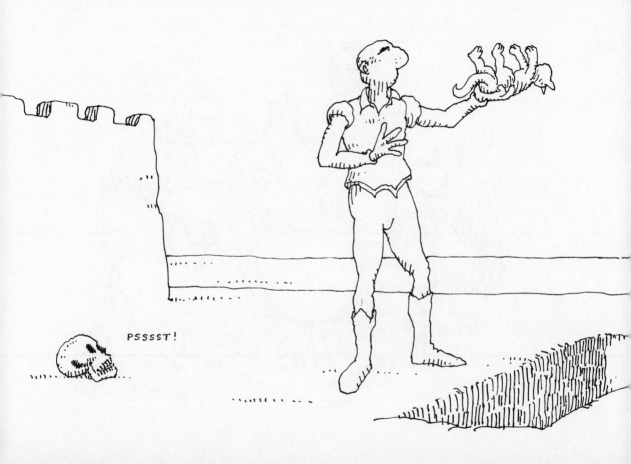

PSSSST!

'Er . . . do you have anything else?'

1667

ISAAC NEWTON IS REMINDED ABOUT GRAVITY

GULLIVER MAKES ANOTHER DISCOVERY

1752

'It's got a message, Master . . . but I don't think we should touch it.'

G.C.Cruikshank fecit...

MONSTROSITIES of 1821

Pub.ᵈ by G.Humphrey 27 St James St London May 20 1821

OLIVER DOES NOT ASK FOR MORE

1871

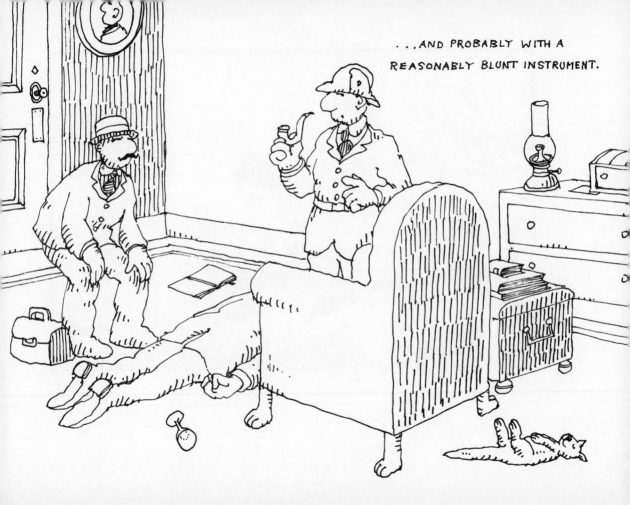

MOSCOW 1917

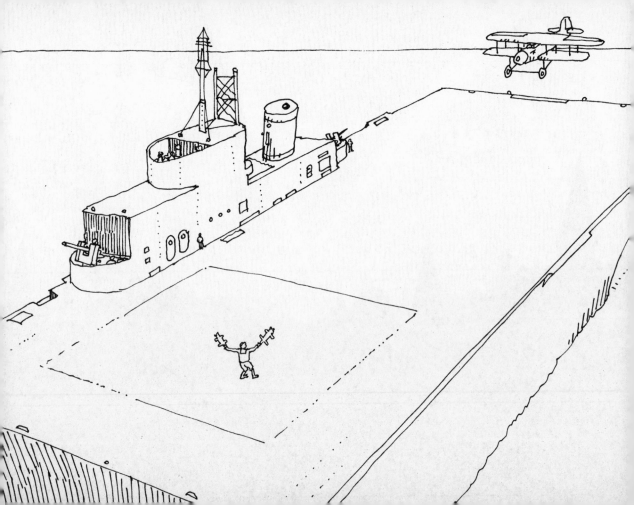

DIMBO

MILLMAN'S DEAD CAT MUSEUM & CURIO SHOPPE (WOOLALOONA FLATS. N.S.W. AUSTRALIA)

FELIX MORT LODGE
TITUSVILLE, NEBRASKA, 1952

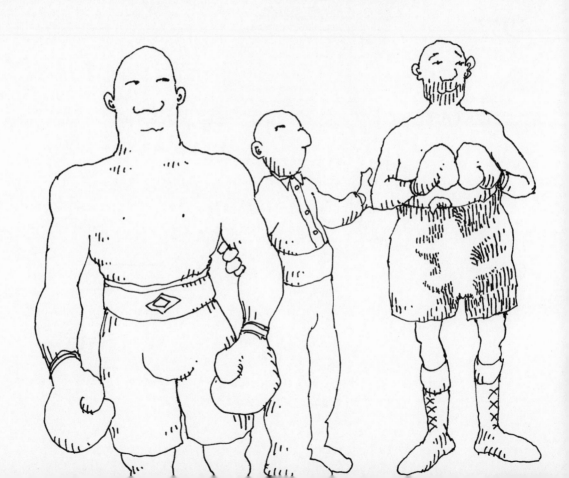

1957

SPUTNIK

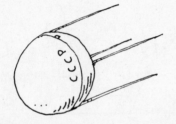

CATNIK

SHE LOVES YOU

YEAH YEAH YEAH....

1979

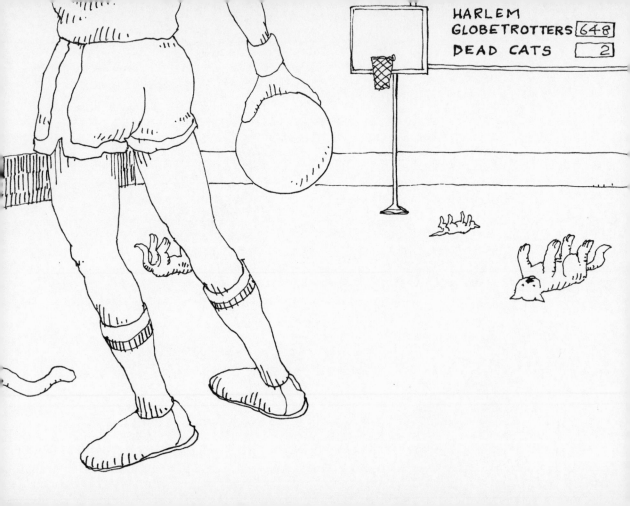

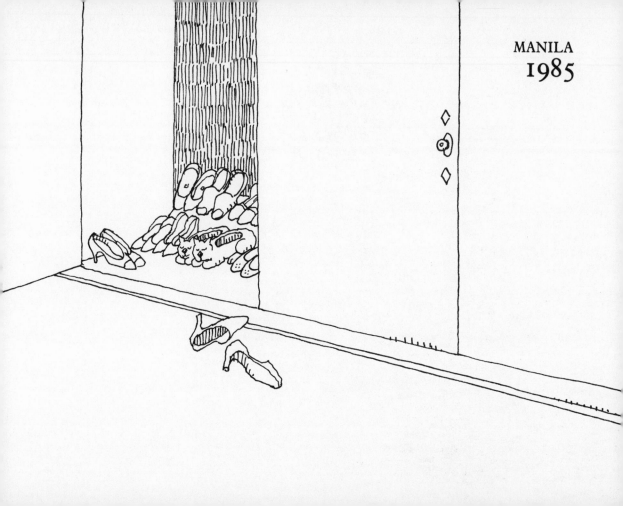

MANILA
1985

1987

BERLIN
1989

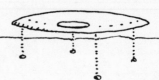

2016

HEY. THESE ARE MY
KIND OF PEOPLE...

I DON'T GET IT.

WHERE'S THE
BATHROOM?